Editor
Torrey K. Maloof

Editor in Chief
Karen J. Goldfluss, M.S. Ed.

Creative Director
Sarah M. Fournier

Cover Artist
Sarah Kim

Illustrator
Mark Mason

Art Coordinator
Renée Mc Elwee

Imaging
Amanda R. Harter

Publisher
Mary D. Smith, M.S. Ed.

LET'S GET THIS DAY STARTED
Math
GRADE 5

TCR 8245

- Start the day off right with engaging standards-based mathematics
- Over 100 pages of activities organized by mathematical concepts, such as numerical expressions, fractions, measurement & data, and geometry
- Activities help improve mathematical reasoning skills and prepare students for real-world problem solving
- Written response questions conclude each section allowing students to assess their own learning and reflect on their mathematical skills

Teacher Created Resources

Author
Pamela Brunskill

Teacher Created Resources
12621 Western Avenue
Garden Grove, CA 92841
www.teachercreated.com
ISBN: 978-1-4206-8245-8
© 2019 Teacher Created Resources
Made in U.S.A.

Teacher Created Resources

Table of Contents

Introduction

Mathematics can be tough for teachers to teach and even tougher for students to learn. Math is not always a fan favorite among the elementary school crowd. It can be intimidating and frustrating. The *Let's Get This Day Started* series is designed to provide students with frequent opportunities to master and retain important math skills in a simple, user-friendly manner.

This book is designed to reinforce key mathematics skills taught in the classroom. As students become active learners in discovering mathematical relationships, they acquire a necessary understanding that improves their problem-solving skills and, therefore, boosts their confidence in math. When using this book, consider incorporating these activities with the actual curriculum that you may be currently using in your classroom. This provides students with a greater chance of mastering math skills and ultimately being successful in college, career, and life.

The activities in this book do not need to be completed every day or even every other day. Teachers should not feel restricted by a daily warm-up or introductory activity. Sometimes, schedules change. A morning assembly, a make-up lesson, or just an extra-busy day can easily throw off a classroom schedule for days. Teachers never know what their days or weeks are going to look like. This book is written so that teachers can stop wherever and whenever they want. They can take their time and arrange the activities to fit their own schedules. They may choose to do a section a day, or spread it out over a week or two. There is no right or wrong way.

This book is divided into units based on different mathematical-content strands. Each unit consists of activities focused on a topic related to that particular strand. A whole-class introductory sheet kicks off each section, followed by a paired-learning activity sheet, and then an independent-learning assessment. Each section concludes with a written response to a prompt that incorporates the topic studied in the section.

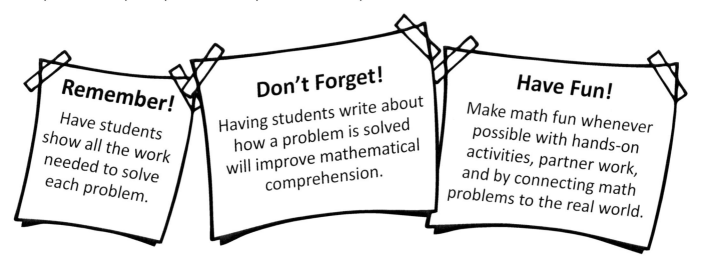

Remember! Have students show all the work needed to solve each problem.

Don't Forget! Having students write about how a problem is solved will improve mathematical comprehension.

Have Fun! Make math fun whenever possible with hands-on activities, partner work, and by connecting math problems to the real world.

All the activities in the *Let's Get This Day Started* series have been aligned to the Common Core State Standards (CCSS). Visit *http://www.teachercreated.com/standards/* for all standards correlations.

How to Use This Book

The first page in each section is the *Read & Learn* page. This page introduces the mathematical topic that will be covered in the section. It breaks down the basics of the mathematical concept by using simple sentences, diagrams, and examples. This page should be a whole-class activity. The teacher should read and review the page with students out loud, answering any questions they may have. These introductory pages can then be saved in a folder and used as study guides, homework helpers, or "cheat sheets."

The second page in each section is the *Partner & Practice* page. This page includes problems for students to solve with a partner. Working collaboratively will provide students with additional guidance and support. Teachers should place students into heterogeneous or homogenous pairs, and circulate around the room as students work together to solve the problems on the page. Teachers should check for understanding and be sure that each student in every pair is actively involved and fully invested in the work. Be sure students show all the work needed to solve each problem. When pairs have finished the page, go over the answers as a class.

The third page in each section is the *Focus & Find* page. This page includes problems for students to solve independently. This page can be completed in class or assigned as homework, and can be used to assess student understanding. Again, be sure students show all the work needed to solve each problem. If students struggle to complete the problems correctly, teachers may choose to supplement with additional learning activities and problems.

The fourth, and final, page in each section is the *Think & Write* page. This page includes writing prompts to help students reflect on the mathematical concept and put their understanding into words. It provides them with opportunities to review, confirm, and reinforce their learning as well as write about how math prolems are solved. Students can save these pages and use them to create a math journal to help them review and study for quizzes and exams.

Read & Learn	Partner & Practice	Focus & Find	Think & Write
	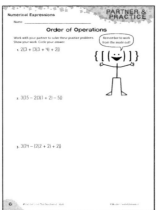		

Name: _____

Order of Operations

We use PEMDAS to remember the order of operations in math problems:

Parentheses

Exponents

Multiplication

Division

Addition

Subtraction

$41 - 20 - 5 + (13 - 3) =$ _____

$41 - 20 - 5 + 10 =$ _____

$16 + 10 =$ _____

26

But what do we do when we have parentheses, brackets, *and* braces?

$$2\{10 [5 + 2(25 - 9) - 20] \}$$

Remember!
A number written next to parentheses means "multiply."

$2(3) = 2 \times 3$

1st **Parentheses ( )**

$25 - 9 = 16$

2nd **Brackets [ ]**

$2 \times 16 + 5 - 20 = 17$

3rd **Braces { }**

$10 \times 17 = 170$

$2 \times 170 = 340$

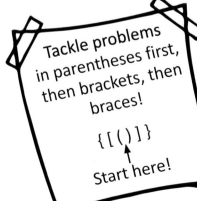
Tackle problems in parentheses first, then brackets, then braces!

$\{ [( )] \}$

Start here!

Name: _____

Order of Operations

Work with your partner to solve these practice problems. Show your work. Circle your answer.

Remember to work from the inside out!

1. $2\{3 + [3(3 + 4) + 2]\}$

2. $3\{15 - 2[3(1 + 2) - 5]\}$

3. $3\{14 - [2(2 + 2) + 2]\}$

Name: _____

Order of Operations

Focus on what you learned. Find the answers. Remember to show your work and circle your answers.

1. $7 + \{3 + [3(2 \times 4)] + 2\}$ 2. $3\{1 + [4(2 + 1) + 3]\}$

Write problems that use a combination of parentheses, brackets, or braces and result in the answer listed in the box. Solve the problem to check your work.

3. [= 10]   4. [= 24]

Challenge: On the back of this sheet, use numbers to write and solve a problem that includes:

☐ two sets of parentheses

☐ one set of brackets

☐ one set of braces

Name: _____

Order of Operations

Think about the order of operations. Write about what you learned.

1. Explain the order in which you would solve this problem.

$$5\{11 - [4(4 - 1) - 1]\}$$

_____

_____

_____

_____

2. Torriana said the answer to the question above is 15. Is she correct, or did she make a mistake? Explain your thinking.

_____

_____

_____

_____

_____

3. In one brief sentence, summarize what you learned in this section.

_____

_____

Name: _____

Simple Expressions

Did you know we can write simple expressions without solving them?

Yes, we really can!

We do this by turning words into numbers.

It's not magic—it's math!

Let's try!

How do we write "four times the sum of three and six"?

$$4(3 + 6)$$

How do we write "the difference of twenty-one and seven divided by two"?

$$(21 - 7) \div 2$$

We can also interpret simple expressions without solving them.

For example: 3(10,000 + 500) is 3 times as large as 10,000 + 500

For simple expressions, we think about how we would solve the problem **and** what the numbers mean.

Simple Expressions

Work with your partner to solve these practice problems. Write the numerical expressions.

1. twenty times the difference of five and two

_____

2. the sum of fifty divided by ten and twenty times the difference of five and two

_____

3. the sum of twenty and ten divided by five

_____

Work with your partner to make a statement about the following numerical expressions.

4. 4(500 + 18) is _____ times as large as 500 + 18.

5. 3(60 – 4)

_____

_____

_____

Name: _____

Simple Expressions

Focus on what you learned. Find the answers.

1. Write the numerical expression for twenty-three times the sum of three, sixteen, and fifty.

_____

2. Write the numerical expression for three times the quotient of six and two.

_____

3. Write the following numerical expression as words: $52(515 - 24)$.

_____

_____

4. What can you infer about $(515 - 24) \div 4$?

_____

_____

5. Write a numerical expression for the following word problem.

Cade made twenty treats for the class party. Yilin and Jalin each brought six treats. The teacher divided the treats into groups of three.

_____

_____

Name: _____

Simple Expressions

Think about simple expressions. Write about what you learned.

1. How do you write "fifty times the sum of two, seven, and five" as a numerical expression? How do you know?

_____

_____

_____

2. Write a word problem about you and your best friend that would fit the numerical expression $12 - (2 \times 3 - 4)$.

_____

_____

_____

_____

3. I (enjoy/do not enjoy) simple expressions because _____

_____

_____

_____

READ &
LEARN

Name: _____

Powers of Ten

How does a number's position tell us its value?

A digit in one place is 10 times the value of the digit to its right.

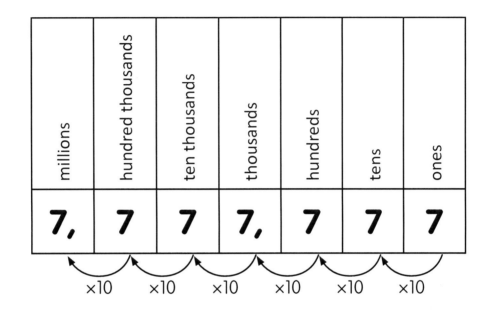

| The 7 in the hundreds place represents 700. | The 7 in the tens place represents 70. |

Likewise, a digit in one place is $\frac{1}{10}$ of the value of the digit to its left.

So, a 7 in the tens place is $\frac{1}{10}$ the value of a 7 in the hundreds place.

5 millions, 6 hundred thousands, 0 ten thousands, 2 thousands, 8 hundreds, 9 tens, 1 one

Name: _____

Powers of Ten

Work with your partner to solve these practice problems.

1. $5,000,000 + 300,000 + 50,000 + 2,000 + 100 + 7 =$ _____

2. 4 thousands + _____ + 9 tens + 5 ones = 4,395

3. Circle the digit that represents $\frac{1}{10}$ of the digit in the thousands place.

   ## 5,555,555

4. How will the value of 9,289,345 change if the number 8 is replaced by the number 1?

   _____

5. Look at the number below. How much will the number decrease if the number 4 is replaced by the number 1?

   ## 4,562,389

   _____

Name: _____

Powers of Ten

Focus on what you learned. Find the answers.

1. Put the following labels in the correct spot in the table:
   hundred thousands, ones, ten thousands, millions, thousands, hundreds, tens

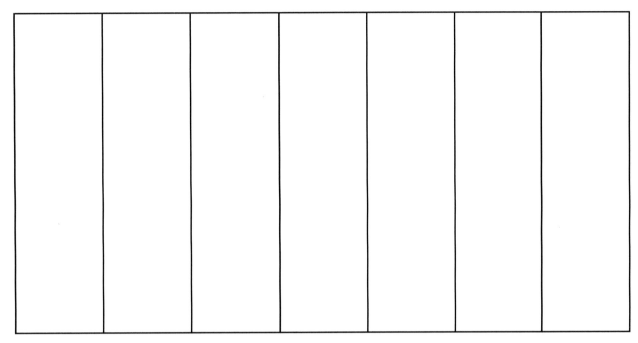

2. Which place value represents 10 times more than the hundred thousands place?

   _____

3. 563,429 = _____ + 6 ten thousands
   + 3 thousands + 4 hundreds + 2 tens + 9 ones

4. How will the value of 18,246,310 change if the number 6 is replaced by the number 5?

   _____

5. 6 hundred thousands + 9 tens + 5 ones = _____

Name: _____

Powers of Ten

Think about the powers of ten in place value. Write about what you learned.

1. Why do you think a digit in one place represents 10 times as much as it represents in the place to its right, and $\frac{1}{10}$ of what it represents in the place to its left? You may want to include a drawing to help illustrate your point.

_____

_____

_____

_____

2. Which of the following numbers have 2 hundred thousands? How do you know?

   125,380   225,890   3,256,421   12,456,001

_____

_____

_____

_____

3. What is the most interesting thing you learned about the powers of ten?

_____

_____

Name: _____

Read and Write Decimals

> Place value can help us read and write decimals.

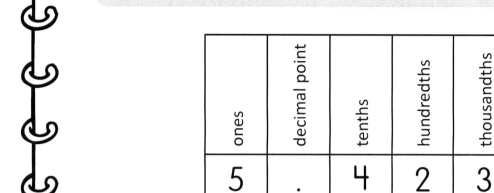

A place-value chart can represent decimals.

$\overleftarrow{\underline{\text{Left}}}$ of the decimal is the larger value.

$\overrightarrow{\underline{\text{Right}}}$ of the decimal is the smaller value.

There are different ways to write decimals.

<u>Standard Form</u>: 5.423

<u>Expanded Form</u>: $5 \times 1 + 4(\frac{1}{10}) + 2(\frac{1}{100}) + 3(\frac{1}{1000})$

<u>Word Form</u>: five and four hundred twenty-three thousandths

Name: _____

Read and Write Decimals

Work with your partner to solve these practice problems.

For questions 1–3, complete the table.

	Standard Form	Expanded Form	Word Form
1.	4.254		four and two hundred fifty-four thousandths
2.		$3 \times 1 + 7(\frac{1}{10}) + 1(\frac{1}{1,000})$	three and seven hundred one thousandths
3.	10.268	$10 \times 1 + 2(\frac{1}{10}) + 6(\frac{1}{100}) + 8(\frac{1}{1,000})$	

4. Write four hundred three thousandths in the place value chart below.

	.			

5. What are two different ways to represent 0.32?

_____

_____

Name: _____

Read and Write Decimals

Focus on what you learned. Find the answers.

Write the following numbers in standard form.

1. five and sixteen hundredths	**2.** nine and three hundred thousandths

Write the following numbers in expanded form.

3. four and sixteen hundredths	**4.** five hundred fifteen thousandths

5. Write $9 \times 1 + 2(\frac{1}{10}) + 3(\frac{1}{100}) + 5(\frac{1}{1,000})$ in the place value chart below.

	•			

Name: _____

Read and Write Decimals

1. How many thousandths are in 1? How do you know?

_____

_____

_____

2. What does *and* stand for when reading number names? Why is it important?

_____

_____

_____

3. When it comes to reading and writing decimals, I am (confident/not confident)

because _____

_____

_____

Name: _____

Rounding Decimals

We know how to round whole numbers.

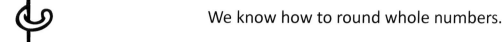

Round to the nearest **ten**.	Round to the nearest **hundred**.
6 → 10	252 → 300
14 → 10	419 → 400
278 → 280	2,542 → 2,500

But, what do we do when we have less than a whole number?

We still round to the closest number!

Number lines can help us round decimals.

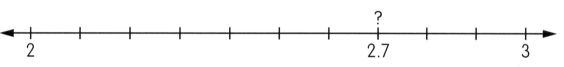

2.7 rounded to the nearest whole number is 3.

Let's round 2.67 to the nearest **tenth**.

2.67 rounded to the nearest tenth is 2.7.

Remember!

If the rounding digit is between 5 and 9, round up. If the rounding digit is between 0 and 4, round down.

Name: _____

Rounding Decimals

Work with your partner to solve these practice problems. Use the number line to help you.

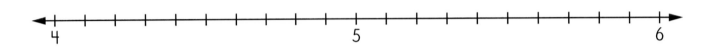

Round the following numbers to the nearest whole number.

1.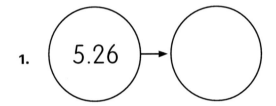

2. (5.09) →

Round the following numbers to the nearest tenth.

3.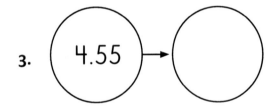

4. (4.00) →

Round the following numbers to the nearest hundredth.

5.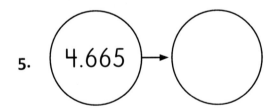

6. (5.999) →

Name: _____

Rounding Decimals

Focus on what you learned. Find the answers. Use the number line to help you.

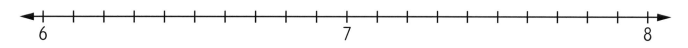

Round the following numbers to the nearest tenth.

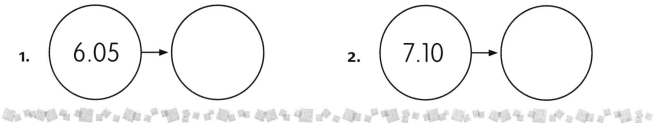

1. 6.05 →

2. 7.10 →

Round the following numbers to the nearest hundredth.

3. 7.223 →

4. 6.074 →

5. Melanie has to create a cover for her math journal. The journal is 8.213 inches wide. Melanie's ruler only extends to the tenths place. If she wants to be as accurate as her ruler will allow, to what number should she round?

_____ inches

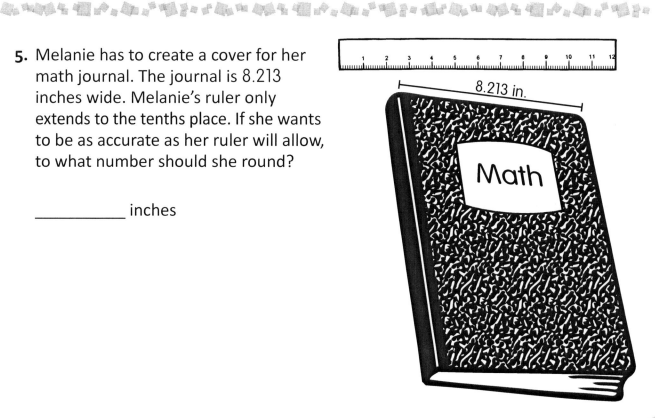

8.213 in.

Math

Name: _____

Rounding Decimals

Think about rounding decimals. Write about what you learned.

1. How do number lines help us round decimals?

_____

_____

_____

2. Draw 15.72 on a number line in the box below. Round it to the nearest tenth. Use words to explain how you arrived at your answer.

_____

_____

_____

3. Write an example of a real-world experience in which you would have to round decimals.

_____

_____

_____

Name: _____

Comparing Decimals

We know how to compare whole numbers.

Symbol	It means...	We use it when...	Example
>	greater than	The first number is **greater than** the second number.	4 > 2
<	less than	The first number is **less than** the second number.	2 < 4
=	equal to	Both numbers are **equal**.	4 = 4

Now, let's compare decimals. To compare decimals, we follow these 3 easy steps!

Step 1   Line up the decimal points.

Step 2   Compare digits from left to right to find the first place where the digits are different.

Step 3   Figure out which digit is greater than (>) or less than (<) the other.

Let's give it a try!

<u>Compare</u>

2.578 and 2.572

1. 2.578
   2.572

2. 2.578
   2.572

   same   different

3. 2.57⑧
   2.57②

2.578 > 2.572

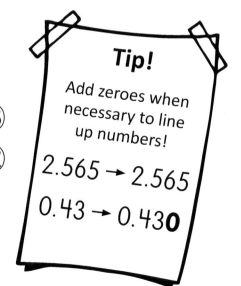

Tip!

Add zeroes when necessary to line up numbers!

2.565 → 2.565

0.43 → 0.43**0**

Name: _____

Comparing Decimals

Work with your partner to solve these practice problems.

For problems 1–3, compare each decimal, using <, >, or =.

1. 3.54 $\bigcirc$ 3.45

2. 0.682 $\bigcirc$ 0.68

3. 2.500 $\bigcirc$ 2.5

4. Yadiel gathered three leaves for his science project. They measured 4.54 inches, 4.892 inches, and 4.57 inches. Use the place value chart below to order them from shortest to longest.

ones	decimal point	tenths	hundredths	thousandths

Decimals

Name: _____

FOCUS & FIND

Comparing Decimals

Focus on what you learned. Find the answers.

For problems 1–3, compare each decimal, using <, >, or =.

1. 3.247 ◯ 3.24

2. 15.682 ◯ 8.999

3. 5.366 ◯ 5.391

4. Ariel organized her seashell collection from smallest to largest. She recorded the lengths in the chart below. Did she order her seashells correctly? Explain why or why not.

ones	decimal point	tenths	hundredths	thousandths
0	.	2	2	5
0	.	2	2	
2	.	3	5	8

seashell collection in centimeters

_____
_____
_____
_____
_____
_____
_____

Name: _____

Comparing Decimals

Think about comparing decimals. Write about what you learned.

1. The first table below shows the number of inches of snow that fell during one week in Buffalo, NY. Reorder the days of snowfall from least to greatest in the second table.

Day	Snow		Day	Snow
Sunday	0.00 in.			
Monday	1.21 in.			
Tuesday	0.5 in.			
Wednesday	4.2 in.			
Thursday	2.25 in.			
Friday	1 in.			
Saturday	1.25 in.			

2. Which day had the least amount of snow? The greatest? How do you know? Explain your reasoning.

_____

_____

_____

_____

3. When I hear someone talk about comparing decimals, I think _____

_____

_____

Name: _____

Adding Decimals

We know how to add whole numbers.

$$\begin{array}{r} 500 \\ + \ 500 \\ \hline 1,000 \end{array}$$

Now, let's add some decimals!

Adding decimals is very similar to adding whole numbers.
We just need to remember three easy steps!

1 Line up the decimals.

2 Bring down the decimal.

3 Add the numbers.

1
$$\begin{array}{r} 5.32 \\ 2.49 \\ +0.48 \end{array}$$
Line up the decimals.

2
$$\begin{array}{r} 5.32 \\ 2.49 \\ +0.48 \end{array}$$
Bring down the decimal.

Don't forget to carry the one!

3
$$\begin{array}{r} 5.32 \\ 2.49 \\ +0.48 \\ \hline 8.29 \end{array}$$
Add the numbers.

Name: _____

Adding Decimals

Work with your partner to solve these practice problems.

1.
$$3.24$$
$$+3.20$$

2.
$$2.56$$
$$1.34$$
$$+5.89$$

3.
$$0.73$$
$$4.21$$
$$+12.04$$

4. $1.1 + 4.69 =$

5. $16.7 + 2.5 + 0.14 =$

Name: _____

Adding Decimals

Focus on what you learned. Find the answers.

1.
$$
\begin{array}{r}
0.89 \\
+1.00 \\
\hline
\end{array}
$$

2.
$$
\begin{array}{r}
0.58 \\
3.04 \\
+1.25 \\
\hline
\end{array}
$$

3. $1.11 + 2.22 + 4.44 =$

4. $0.50 + 2.17 + 3.2 =$

5. Neri loves his dog. He bought dog treats that cost $2.50, a new leash that cost $24.99, and a chew toy for 75¢. How much money did he spend in total? Show your work below. Write your answer in the dog bone below.

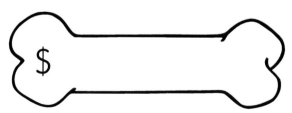

Name: _____

Adding Decimals

Think about adding decimals. Write about what you learned.

1. Mr. Pulido asked his students to solve $8.23 + 4.02 + 0.1$. Emilio solved the problem as follows:

$$
\begin{array}{r}
8.23 \\
4.02 \\
+\quad 0.1 \\
\hline
12.26
\end{array}
$$

What advice would you give to Emilio? Is this answer correct? Why, or why not?

_____

_____

_____

_____

2. Sally and Lia were baking cupcakes. They needed 2 cups of sugar. Sally found 1.6 cups of sugar. Lia found 0.6 cups of sugar. Did they have enough sugar for the recipe? Use words to explain your reasoning.

_____

_____

_____

3. I will need to know how to add decimals in my everyday life when I _____

_____

_____

Name: _____

Subtracting Decimals

We know how to subtract multi-digit whole numbers.

$$
\begin{array}{r}
\overset{4\ \ 14}{\cancel{5}\,\cancel{4}\,7} \\
-\ 2\,5\,5 \\
\hline
2\,9\,2
\end{array}
$$

Subtracting decimals is similar. We can do it in three simple steps!

$$47.32 - 15.25$$

Step 1 Line up the decimals.

Step 2 Bring down the decimal point.

Step 3 Subtract each column. Start on the right and move to the left.

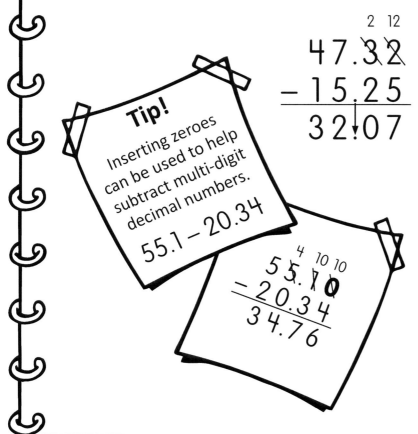

$$
\begin{array}{r}
\overset{2\ \ 12}{47.3\,\cancel{2}} \\
-\ 15.25 \\
\hline
32.07
\end{array}
$$

Tip!
Inserting zeroes can be used to help subtract multi-digit decimal numbers.

$$55.1 - 20.34$$

$$
\begin{array}{r}
\overset{4\ \ 10\ 10}{5\,5.\,\cancel{1}\,\cancel{0}} \\
-\ 2\,0.3\,4 \\
\hline
3\,4.7\,6
\end{array}
$$

Name: _____

Subtracting Decimals

Work with your partner to solve these practice problems.

1.
$$\begin{array}{r} 7.2 \\ -3.7 \\ \hline \end{array}$$

2.
$$\begin{array}{r} 12.8 \\ -\ 0.4 \\ \hline \end{array}$$

3. $5 - 2.05 =$

4. $6.3 - 2.53 =$

5. Marco has $15. He spends $3.75 on a bag of dog treats. How much money does he have left? Show your work.

Name: _____

Subtracting Decimals

Focus on what you learned. Find the answers.

1.
$$\begin{array}{r} 2.34 \\ -0.59 \\ \hline \end{array}$$

2.
$$\begin{array}{r} 0.99 \\ -0.91 \\ \hline \end{array}$$

3. $5.34 - 2.1 =$

4. $6.8 - 3.55 =$

5. Theodora has $2. She spends $1.60 on a cookie. How much money does Theodora still have? Show your work.

Name: _____

Subtracting Decimals

Think about subtracting decimals. Write about what you learned.

1. What do you know about subtracting decimals?

_____

_____

_____

2. Why is 14.59 − 12.01 less than 3.01 − 0.06? Use words, numbers, or drawings to explain your answer.

_____

3. I will need to know how to subtract decimals in my everyday life when I _____

_____

_____

Name: _____

Multiplying Decimals

We know how to multiply whole numbers.

$$
\begin{array}{r}
^{1} \\
3\ 2\ 1 \\
\times\ 6\ 1\ 5 \\
\hline
1\ 6\ 0\ 5 \\
3\ 2\ 1\ 0 \\
+1\ 9\ 2\ 6\ 0\ 0 \\
\hline
1\ 9\ 7,4\ 1\ 5
\end{array}
$$

When multiplying decimals, we do the same thing.

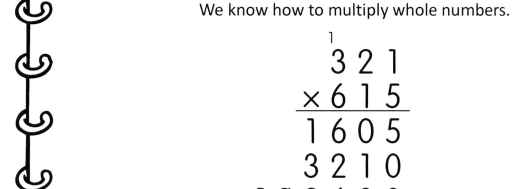

Don't forget to regroup!

$$
\begin{array}{r}
^{1} \\
3.2\ 1 \\
\times\ 6.1\ 5 \\
\hline
1\ 6\ 0\ 5 \\
3\ 2\ 1\ 0 \\
+1\ 9\ 2\ 6\ 0\ 0 \\
\hline
1\ 9\ 7,4\ 1\ 5
\end{array}
$$

Don't forget to include your zeroes!

But, where does the decimal point go?

To find out, we count the number of decimal place "hops" from right to left.

$3.\overset{2\ \ 1}{2\ 1}$ 2 hops

$6.\underset{4\ \ 3}{15}$ $+\ 2$ hops
   $+\ 4$ hops

19.7415
   $4\ 3\ 2\ 1$

4 hops

$$3.21 \times 6.15 = 19.7415$$

Name: _____

Multiplying Decimals

Work with your partner to solve these practice problems.

1. $\begin{array}{r} 7.41 \\ \times\, 2.18 \\ \hline \end{array}$

2. $\begin{array}{r} 0.25 \\ \times\, 0.45 \\ \hline \end{array}$

3. Look at the problem: 8.12×2.01. Guess the answer. Circle your guess.

    1.63212   16.3212   163.212   1,632.12

    Now, solve the problem! Show your work. Did you guess correctly?

4. Lynn buys her dog 6 cans of dog food. Each can weighs 13.2 oz. How many total ounces do all the dog food cans weigh? Show your work.

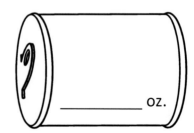

_____ oz.

Name: _____

Multiplying Decimals

Focus on what you learned. Find the answers.

1.
$$\begin{array}{r} 0.7 \\ \times\, 0.3 \\ \hline \end{array}$$

2.
$$\begin{array}{r} 1.6 \\ \times\, 4 \\ \hline \end{array}$$

3. $5.6 \times 10 =$

4. $22.45 \times 10.32 =$

5. Write a word problem in which you multiply decimals. Solve the problem on the back of this sheet.

_____

_____

_____

THINK &
WRITE

Name: _____

Multiplying Decimals

Think about multiplying decimals. Write about what you learned.

1. How is multiplying decimals similar to multiplying whole numbers? How is it different?

_____

_____

_____

_____

2. If $28 \times 9 = 252$, what would $2.8 \times 0.9 = ?$ How could you find this answer without writing the problem out?

_____

_____

_____

3. I (like/dislike) multiplying decimals because _____

_____

_____

_____

Name: _____

Dividing Decimals

When we divide whole numbers, we:

divide → multiply → subtract → bring down

$$
\begin{array}{r}
3 \leftarrow \text{quotient} \\
\text{divisor} \rightarrow 21\overline{)63} \leftarrow \text{dividend} \\
-63 \\
\hline
0
\end{array}
$$

We follow similar steps when we divide with decimals...
but with a few small changes.

If the decimal is in the dividend, we move it up.

$$2\overline{)5{.}2}$$

Then, solve for the quotient.

$$
\begin{array}{r}
2.6 \\
2\overline{)5.2} \\
-4\downarrow \\
\hline
1\,2 \\
-1\,2 \\
\hline
0
\end{array}
$$

If the decimal is in the divisor, we move it to the right to make it a whole number.

$$0{.}5\overline{)2}$$

Then, we move the decimal in the dividend the same number of times. We may need to add zeroes

$$0{.}5\overline{)2{.}0}$$

Now, we move the decimal up and solve.

$$
\begin{array}{r}
4.0 \\
5\overline{)20{.}0} \\
-20 \\
\hline
0
\end{array}
$$

Let's try one more!

$$2{.}1\overline{)2{.}52}$$

$$21\overline{)25{.}2}$$

$$
\begin{array}{r}
1.2 \\
21\overline{)25.2} \\
-21\downarrow \\
\hline
4\,2 \\
-4\,2 \\
\hline
0
\end{array}
$$

Name: _____

Dividing Decimals

Work with your partner to solve these practice problems.

1. $0.8 \overline{)8}$

2. $0.2 \overline{)56}$

3. $0.04 \overline{)2.08}$

4. $4.2 \overline{)6.3}$

5. $1.6 \overline{)42.8}$

6. $3.2 \overline{)81.92}$

Name: _____

Dividing Decimals

Focus on what you learned. Find the answers.

1. $1.5\overline{)3}$

2. $0.65\overline{)3.12}$

3. $1.32\overline{)6.6}$

4. $0.25\overline{)24.75}$

5. $3.6\overline{)9}$

2. $0.75\overline{)4.65}$

Name: _____

Dividing Decimals

Think about dividing decimals. Write about what you learned.

1. Why do you think it is a good idea to make the divisor a whole number when dividing decimals?

_____

_____

_____

2. Would $24.75 \div 0.25$ and $247.5 \div 2.5$ give you the same or different answers? How do you know?

_____

_____

_____

3. I think the most important thing to remember about dividing decimals is _____

_____

_____

_____

Name: _____

Adding Fractions

How do we add fractions with unlike denominators?

$$\frac{1}{3} + \frac{4}{7} = ?$$

We use equivalent fractions to form a common denominator!

$$\frac{1}{3} \times \frac{7}{7} = \frac{7}{21} \qquad\qquad \frac{4}{7} \times \frac{3}{3} = \frac{12}{21}$$

The least common denominator for $\frac{1}{3}$ and $\frac{4}{7}$ is 21.

Now, we can add the fractions.

$$\frac{7}{21} + \frac{12}{21} = \frac{19}{21}$$

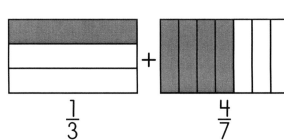

$$\frac{1}{3} \qquad\qquad \frac{4}{7}$$

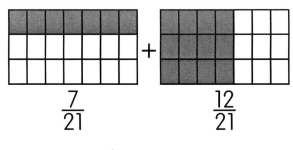

$$\frac{7}{21} \qquad\qquad \frac{12}{21}$$

Tip!

To find the least common denominator, look at multiples of the denominators of fractions you are adding.

For $\frac{1}{3}$, multiples of 3 include 3, 6, 9, 12, 15, 18, ⓛ21, and so on.

For $\frac{4}{7}$, multiples of 7 include 7, 14, ⓛ21, 28, 35, and so on.

21 is the lowest number in common.

If you solve the problem with a higher multiple, you may need to simplify your fraction.

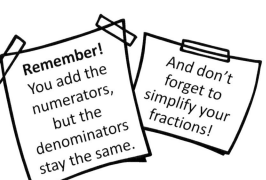

Remember! You add the numerators, but the denominators stay the same.

And don't forget to simplify your fractions!

Name: _____

Adding Fractions

Work with your partner to solve these problems.

1. $\dfrac{2}{5} + \dfrac{3}{7} =$

2. $\dfrac{1}{6} + \dfrac{5}{15} =$

3. $\dfrac{1}{8} + \dfrac{4}{12} =$

4. $\dfrac{1}{3} + \dfrac{2}{5} =$

5. Draw a picture to represent $\dfrac{3}{8} + \dfrac{1}{4}$. Then solve the problem.

Name: _____

Adding Fractions

Focus on what you learned. Find the answers.

1. $\dfrac{1}{4} + \dfrac{2}{3} =$

2. $\dfrac{1}{2} + \dfrac{1}{3} =$

3. $\dfrac{3}{9} + \dfrac{4}{10} =$

4. $\dfrac{1}{8} + \dfrac{3}{4} =$

5. Solve the problem below.

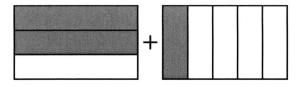

_____

Name: _____

Adding Fractions

Think about adding fractions. Write about what you learned.

1. $\frac{1}{3} +$ _____ $= \frac{8}{15}$. What fraction is missing? How do you know? Show your work in the box. Then, explain in words how you found the answer.

_____

_____

_____

_____

2. Don doesn't know how to add fractions with unlike denominators. Explain the process to him.

_____

_____

_____

_____

3. When I think of adding fractions, I think _____

_____

_____

_____

Name: _____

Subtracting Fractions

When we add fractions with unlike denominators, the first step is to form equivalent fractions.

$$\frac{2}{5} + \frac{1}{4} \longrightarrow \frac{8}{20} + \frac{5}{20}$$

We do the same thing when we subtract!

$$\frac{2}{5} - \frac{1}{4} \longrightarrow \frac{8}{20} - \frac{5}{20}$$

Then, we subtract the numerators.

$$\frac{8}{20} - \frac{5}{20} = \frac{3}{20}$$

When subtracting fractions you must
find common denominators or bust.
For if you don't
the difference won't
be a solution to trust.

A leprechaun's limerick:

Name: _____

Subtracting Fractions

Work with your partner to solve these practice problems.

1. $\dfrac{3}{4} - \dfrac{2}{3} =$

2. $\dfrac{5}{6} - \dfrac{4}{7} =$

3. $\dfrac{3}{5} - \dfrac{2}{8} =$

4. $\dfrac{7}{12} - \dfrac{1}{4} =$

5. $\dfrac{7}{8} - \dfrac{1}{3} =$

6. $\dfrac{5}{7} - \dfrac{3}{5} =$

Name: _____

Subtracting Fractions

Focus on what you learned. Find the answers.

1. $\dfrac{1}{4} - \dfrac{1}{8} =$

2. $\dfrac{8}{9} - \dfrac{3}{4} =$

3. $\dfrac{17}{18} - \dfrac{1}{3} =$

4. $\dfrac{5}{8} - \dfrac{1}{16} =$

5. $\dfrac{2}{3} - \dfrac{2}{7} =$

6. $\dfrac{7}{10} - \dfrac{3}{5} =$

Name: _____

Subtracting Fractions

Think about subtracting fractions. Focus on what you learned

1. Jeff had $\frac{1}{3}$ of a yard of string. He told Timothy that he used $\frac{2}{5}$ of a yard to fix his kite. Timothy told him this was not possible. Is Timothy right? Why, or why not?

_____

_____

_____

_____

2. Joanna said $\frac{4}{13} - \frac{3}{26} = \frac{3}{39}$. Is she correct? Explain your reasoning.

_____

_____

_____

_____

3. I feel that subtracting fractions is _____

_____

_____

_____

Name: _____

Multiplying Fractions

When multiplying fractions, numbers get smaller.

Think of an ice cube melting.

$$\frac{3}{4} \times \frac{2}{5} =$$

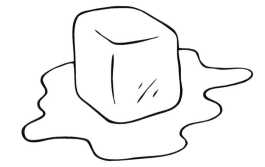

$$\frac{6}{20} = \frac{3}{10}$$

To multiply two fractions, we multiply the numerators and the denominators.

Remember!

Simplify your fractions when necessary.

$$\frac{(3 \times 2)}{(4 \times 5)} = \frac{6}{20} \xrightarrow{\text{(simplify)}} \frac{3}{10}$$

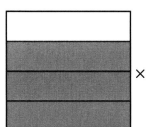 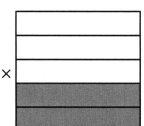

Name: _____

Multiplying Fractions

Work with your partner to solve these practice problems.

1. $\dfrac{3}{4} \times \dfrac{5}{6} =$ _____

2. $\dfrac{1}{3} \times \dfrac{7}{10} =$ _____

3. $\dfrac{8}{9} \times \dfrac{1}{8} =$ _____

4. $\dfrac{1}{2} \times \dfrac{1}{20} =$ _____

5. $\dfrac{10}{11} \times \dfrac{2}{7} =$ _____

Name: _____

Multiplying Fractions

Focus on what you learned. Find the answers. Draw a line to match the answer to the problem.

1. $\dfrac{3}{5} \times \dfrac{4}{7}$

a. $\dfrac{16}{55}$

2. $\dfrac{8}{11} \times \dfrac{2}{5}$

b. $\dfrac{1}{4}$

3. $\dfrac{5}{12} \times \dfrac{1}{4}$

c. $\dfrac{5}{48}$

4. $\dfrac{4}{5} \times \dfrac{1}{2}$

d. $\dfrac{2}{5}$

5. $\dfrac{3}{4} \times \dfrac{1}{3}$

e. $\dfrac{12}{35}$

Name: _____

Multiplying Fractions

Think about multiplying fractions. Write about what you learned.

1. What do you know about multiplying fractions?

_____

_____

_____

2. Write your own multiplication problem with two fractions. Then, solve it.

_____

3. One question I still have about multiplying fractions is _____

_____

_____

_____

Name: _____

Multiplying a Whole Number by a Fraction

How do we multiply a whole number with a fraction?

$$5 \times \frac{1}{3} = ?$$

Look at the table.

There are 5 columns.

But, only $\frac{1}{3}$ of each column is shaded.

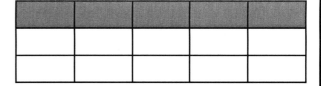

To find the product, we add $\frac{1}{3}$ five times.

$$5 \times \frac{1}{3} = \frac{1}{3} + \frac{1}{3} + \frac{1}{3} + \frac{1}{3} + \frac{1}{3} = \frac{5 \times 1}{3} = \frac{5}{3} = 1\frac{2}{3}$$

Or, we can convert the whole number to a fraction.

To do this, we place the whole number over 1 and then multiply the numerators and the denominators.

$$5 \times \frac{1}{3} = \frac{5}{1} \times \frac{1}{3} = \frac{5}{3}$$

To convert the improper fraction to a mixed number, we divide the numerator by the denominator. Then, we write the remainder over the denominator.

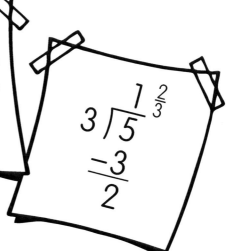

Name: _____

Multiplying a Whole Number by a Fraction

Work with your partner to solve these practice problems.

1. Write this multiplication problem:

_____

2. Solve problem #1 by using repeated addition.

3. Solve #1 by converting the whole number into a fraction.

4. $8 \times \frac{3}{7} =$ _____

5. $\frac{2}{3} \times 9 =$ _____

Name: _____

Multiplying a Whole Number by a Fraction

Focus on what you learned. Find the answers.

1. $5 \times \frac{5}{6} =$ _____

2. $11 \times \frac{3}{5} =$ _____

3. $\frac{7}{8} \times 2 =$ _____

4. $\frac{11}{14} \times 7 =$ _____

5. Draw a figure that represents $3 \times \frac{1}{4}$.

Name: _____

Multiplying a Whole Number by a Fraction

Think about multiplying a whole number by a fraction. Write about what you learned.

1. Why does the following figure NOT represent $\frac{1}{6} \times 5$? Explain.

_____

_____

_____

2. Jamie said whole numbers multiplied by simple fractions are always less than the original whole numbers. Is Jamie correct? Why, or why not?

_____

_____

_____

_____

3. I'm good at multiplying a whole number by a fraction because _____

_____

_____

_____

Name: _____

Dividing a Whole Number by a Fraction

When we divide a whole number by a fraction,
we are finding out how many groups of
the fraction can fit into the whole.

$$4 \div \frac{2}{3} = ?$$

$\frac{4}{1} \div \frac{2}{3}$	**Step 1:** Change the whole number into a fraction.
$\frac{4}{1} \div \frac{3}{2}$	**Step 2:** Flip the numerator and denominator of the original fraction.
$\frac{4}{1} \times \frac{3}{2} = \frac{12}{2}$	**Step 3:** Multiply across.
$\frac{12}{2} \longrightarrow 6$	**Step 4:** Simplify the fraction if necessary.

Fun Fact!

When you divide a whole number by a fraction, the answer is always larger than the original.

Name: _____

Dividing a Whole Number by a Fraction

Work with your partner to solve these practice problems.

1. $6 \div \frac{3}{4} =$

2. $1 \div$ _____ $= \frac{1}{10}$

3. $2 \div \frac{5}{6} =$

4. $4 \div \frac{9}{10} =$

5. $12 \div \frac{2}{3} =$

6. $7 \div \frac{1}{8} =$

Name: _____

Dividing a Whole Number by a Fraction

Focus on what you learned. Find the answers.

1. $4 \div \dfrac{5}{6} =$

2. $5 \div \dfrac{1}{2} =$

3. $6 \div \dfrac{1}{3} =$

4. $2 \div \dfrac{4}{3} =$

5. $3 \div$ _____ $= 6$

Riddle: Which answer above would a gymnast like best? Why?

_____

_____

_____

Name: _____

Dividing a Whole Number by a Fraction

Think about dividing a whole number by a fraction. Write about what you learned.

1. Why is the answer always more than the original when you divide a whole number by a fraction?

_____

_____

_____

2. A gymnast flipping may be one image you could use to help you remember to "flip" the fraction. What is another image you can use to help you remember to flip the fraction? Explain your thinking.

_____

_____

_____

3. When I hear someone say dividing a whole number by a fraction is hard, I think

_____

_____

_____

Name: _____

Conversions

We know how different-size measurement units compare to one another.

1 foot = 12 inches

1 yard = 3 feet

1 mile = 1,760 yards

8 ounces = 1 cup

2 cups = 1 pint

2 pints = 1 quart

But how do we convert among different-sized measurement units?

Big to Small (×)

When converting larger units to smaller units, multiply.

How many feet are in 5 yards?
We know there are 3 feet in 1 yard.

$$3 \times 5 = 15$$

There are 15 feet in 5 yards.

Small to Big (÷)

When converting smaller units to larger units, divide.

How many quarts are in 4 pints?
We know there are 2 pints in 1 quart.

$$4 \div 2 = 2$$

There are 2 quarts in 4 pints.

Name: _____

Conversions

Work with your partner to solve these practice problems. Show your work.

1. How many feet are in 18 inches?

   _____ feet

2. 36 feet = _____ yards

3. 1 mile = _____ feet

4. 97 feet = _____ inches

5. 64 ounces = _____ cups

6. How many quarts are in 6 pints?

   _____ quarts

7. _____ ounces = 4 pints

8. 41 cups = _____ ounces

Name: _____

Conversions

Focus on what you learned. Find the answers. Show your work.

1. 3 feet = _____ inches

2. 5,280 yards = _____ miles

3. How many feet are in 2 miles?

_____ feet

4. 6 feet = _____ yards

5. 24 ounces = _____ cups

6. _____ cup = 4 ounces

7. 1 quart = _____ cups

8. How many cups are in 164 quarts?

_____ cups

Name: _____

Conversions

Think about conversions. Write about what you learned.

1. Explain in words how to convert inches to yards.

_____

_____

_____

_____

_____

2. Which is longer: a playground that is 100 yards long or a playground that is 0.5 miles long? How do you know? Explain.

_____

_____

_____

3. Write about a real-life situation where you would need to convert different-sized measurement units.

_____

_____

_____

Name: _____

Line Plots

We know how to display data in a line plot.

Number of baseball games Mr. Fischer's students played last week	
games played	number of students
0	4
1	5
2	3
3	1

Baseball Games Played Last Week

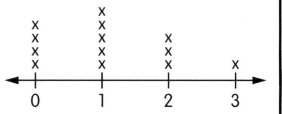

But, how do we display a data set of measurements in fractions of a unit?

The heights of Mr. Fischer's students in inches are:

$57, 54, 54\frac{1}{4}, 56\frac{3}{4}, 57, 55, 54, 56\frac{3}{4}, 54, 55\frac{1}{2}$

First, we organize the data. We write it in order from least to greatest, or we can place the data in a table.

$54, 54, 54, 54\frac{1}{4}, 55, 55\frac{1}{2}, 56\frac{3}{4}, 56\frac{3}{4}, 57, 57$

Height of Students in Mr. Fischer's Class	
Height (inches)	Number of Students
54	3
$54\frac{1}{4}$	1
55	1
$55\frac{1}{2}$	1
$56\frac{3}{4}$	2
57	2

Height of Students in Mr. Fischer's Class

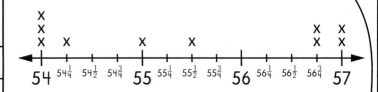

Then, we convert the data to a line plot. Be sure to add the required number of hash marks. In this case, you need $\frac{1}{4}$ marks.

* Don't forget to add a title to your line plot.

Name: _____

Line Plots

Work with your partner to solve these practice problems.

1. Organize the following data measured in inches, from smallest to largest:
$3, 2\frac{1}{2}, 1\frac{3}{4}, 2, 2\frac{1}{2}, 2\frac{3}{4}, \frac{1}{2}$

2. Draw a line plot for the above data.

3. What measurement appeared most often? _____

4. Draw a line plot for the following data about rainfall in Jupiter, Florida, in a given week.

Sunday	2.5 inches
Monday	0 inches
Tuesday	0.5 inches
Wednesday	1 inch
Thursday	1.25 inches
Friday	1 inch
Saturday	1 inch

5. What would be a good title for this line plot?

_____

Name: _____

Line Plots

Focus on what you learned. Find the answers.

1. The students in Mrs. Hader's class had a competition. They wanted to see how far students could jump in feet. Nine students participated in the contest.

   Organize the data from smallest to largest. ⟶

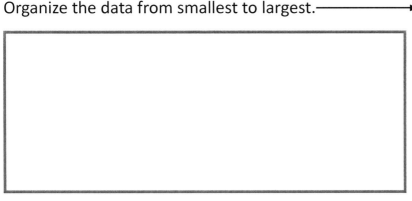

$3\frac{3}{4}$ 4

5    $4\frac{1}{2}$

4   5

3    $4\frac{3}{4}$

$3\frac{1}{4}$

2. Plot the data on a line plot.

3. Write a title on your line plot.

4. How many more students jumped 5 feet than 3 feet? _____

Name: _____

Line Plots

Think about line plots. Write about what you learned.

1. Why is it a good idea to organize data before plotting it?

_____

_____

2. What is different about using data sets on line plots that only have whole numbers and data sets that have fractions? Write and draw your response.

_____

_____

_____

```
┌─────────────────────────────────────────────────────────────┐
│                                                               │
│                                                               │
│                                                               │
│                                                               │
│                                                               │
│                                                               │
└─────────────────────────────────────────────────────────────┘
```

3. I (like/dislike) working with line plots because _____

_____

_____

_____

Geometry

Name: _____

Classifying 2-D Figures

When classifying 2-D figures, we need to pay attention to sides and angles.

Right Triangle
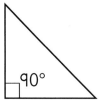

3 sides
1 right angle (90°)

Acute Triangle

3 sides
3 acute angles (<90°)

Obtuse Triangle
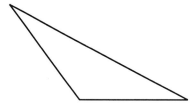

3 sides
1 obtuse angle (>90°)

Parallelogram
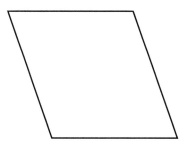

4 sides (opposite sides parallel
and of equal length)
Opposite angles are equal

Square
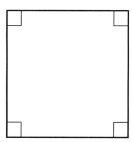

4 sides of equal length
4 right angles

Rectangle

4 sides (opposite sides parallel
and of equal length)
4 right angles

Rhombus
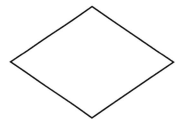

4 sides of equal length
Angles can be any degrees
Opposite angles are equal

Name: _____

Classifying 2-D Figures

Work with your partner to solve these practice problems. Use the Word Bank to identify each figure.

Word Bank	right triangle	acute triangle	rhombus
	parallelogram	rectangle	square

1. _____

2. _____

3. _____

4. _____

5. _____

6. _____

Name: _____

Classifying 2-D Figures

Focus on what you learned. Find the answers.

Draw examples of the following figures. Use the right angle symbol (¬) to identify 90° angles.

1. acute triangle

2. square

3. parallelogram

4. right triangle

5. rectangle

6. obtuse triangle

Name: _____

Classifying 2-D Figures

Think about classifying 2-D figures. Write about what you learned.

1. How do you classify a 2-D figure?

_____

_____

_____

2. What is the difference between an acute triangle and an obtuse triangle?

_____

_____

_____

_____

3. What is your favorite 2-D figure? Why?

_____

_____

_____

Name: _____

Coordinate Planes

Coordinate planes use two perpendicular number lines that intersect at 0.

We call the vertical line *y*.

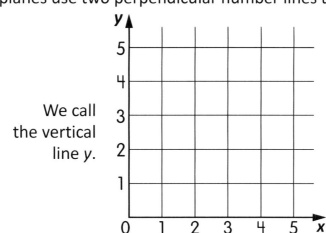

We call the horizontal number line *x*.

When plotting coordinate pairs:

— the first number indicates how far to travel on the *x*-axis.

— the second number indicates how far to travel on the *y*-axis.

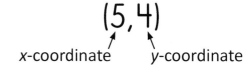

(5, 4)

x-coordinate   *y*-coordinate

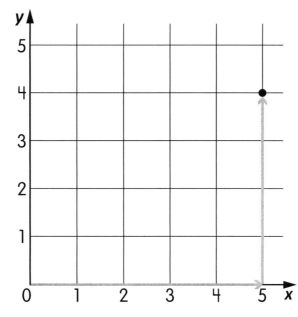

To plot (5, 4), we start at 0 and go over 5 and up 4.

Name: _____

Coordinate Planes

Work with your partner to solve these practice problems.

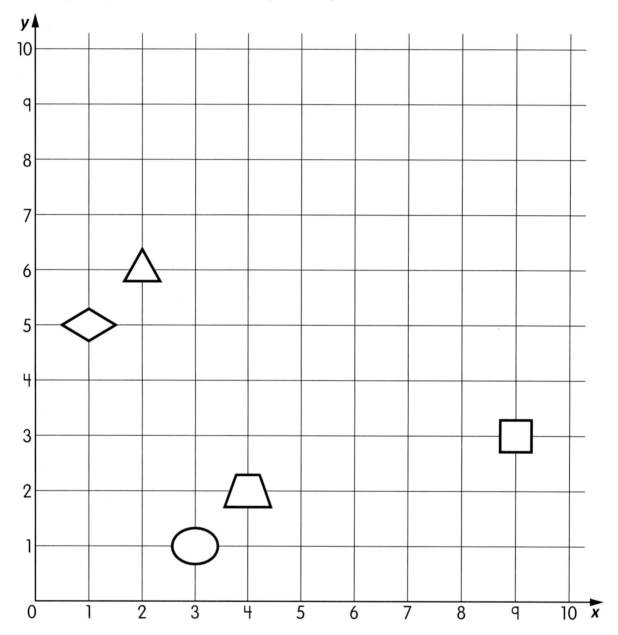

What shape do you find at the following coordinates?

1. (1, 5) _____

2. (3, 1) _____

3. (4, 2) _____

4. (9, 3) _____

5. (2, 6) _____

Defy Gravity: Put a star at (9, 9)!

Name: _____

Coordinate Planes

Focus on what you learned. Plot a point at the following coordinate pairs.

1. (3, 8)   **2.** (6, 8)   **3.** (8, 8)   **4.** (6, 5)   **5.** (6, 2)

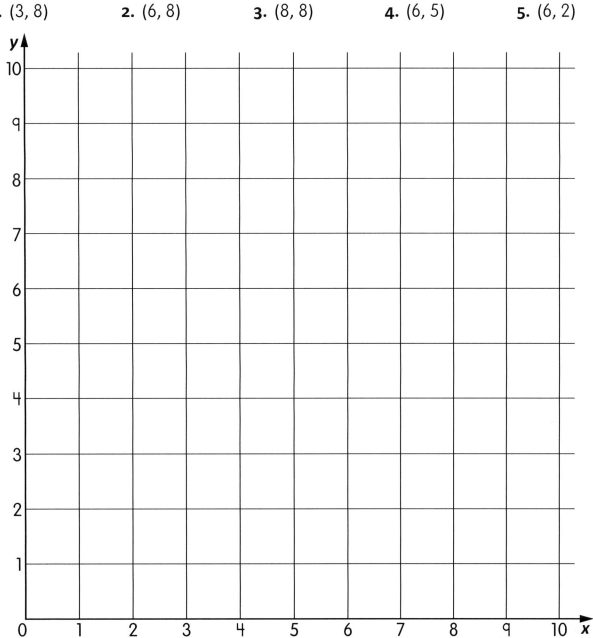

Flying High: If you connect all the coordinate pairs on the grid, what letter do they create?

_____

Name: _____

Coordinate Planes

Think about coordinate planes. Write about what you learned.

1. What do you know about coordinate pairs and coordinate planes?

   _____

   _____

   _____

2. Look at how Lisa plotted (6, 4) on the coordinate plane. What advice would you give her?

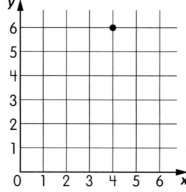

   _____

   _____

   _____

3. When I think of coordinate planes, I feel _____

   _____

   _____

   _____

Name: _____

Volume

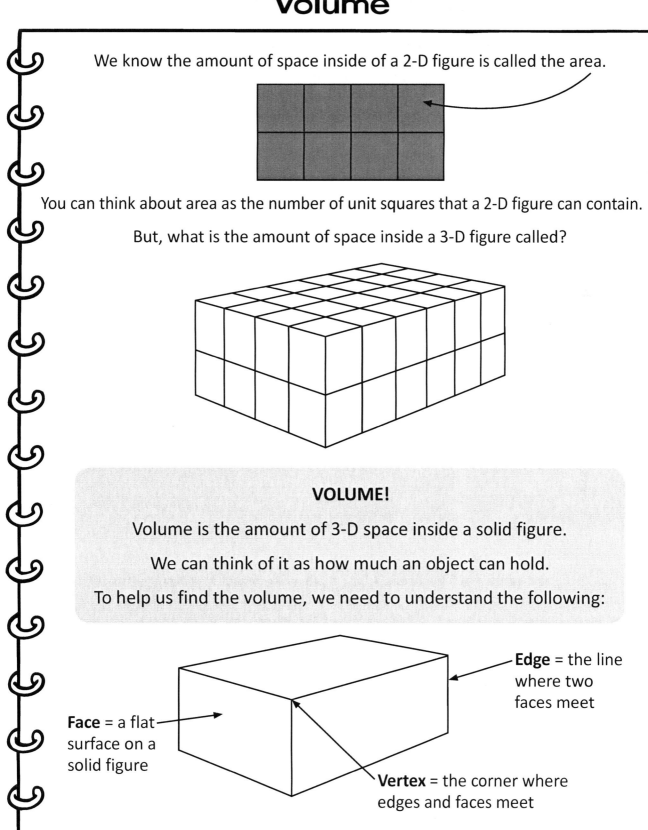

We know the amount of space inside of a 2-D figure is called the area.

You can think about area as the number of unit squares that a 2-D figure can contain.

But, what is the amount of space inside a 3-D figure called?

VOLUME!

Volume is the amount of 3-D space inside a solid figure.

We can think of it as how much an object can hold.

To help us find the volume, we need to understand the following:

Edge = the line where two faces meet

Face = a flat surface on a solid figure

Vertex = the corner where edges and faces meet

This rectangular prism has 6 faces, 12 edges, and 8 vertices.

Name: _____

Volume

Work with your partner to solve these practice problems.

1. Circle the objects for which you can find the volume.

Use the drawing below to answer the questions.

2. What does the star on the prism indicate? _____.

3. What does the heart on the prism indicate? _____.

4. What does the smiley face on the prism indicate? _____.

5. How many faces are in this prism? _____

Geometric Measurements

Name: _____

Volume

Focus on what you learned. Find the answers.

1. Circle the objects for which you can find the volume.

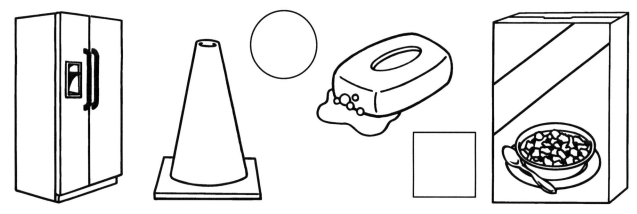

Identify the number of faces, edges, and vertices for each figure.

2. Cube

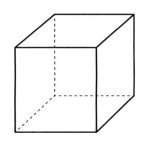

_____ faces, _____ edges,

and _____ vertices

3. Rectangular Prism

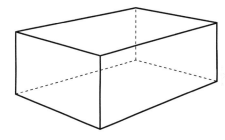

_____ faces, _____ edges,

and _____ vertices

4. Triangular Prism

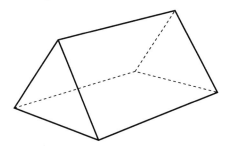

_____ faces, _____ edges, and _____ vertices

Geometric Measurements

Name: _____

Volume

Think about volume. Write about what you learned.

1. Which object has the greater volume? Why?

_____

_____

_____

2. Why do rectangular prisms and cubes always have the same number of faces, edges, and vertices?

_____

_____

_____

3. When I think of volume, I think _____

_____

_____

Name: _____

Measuring Volume

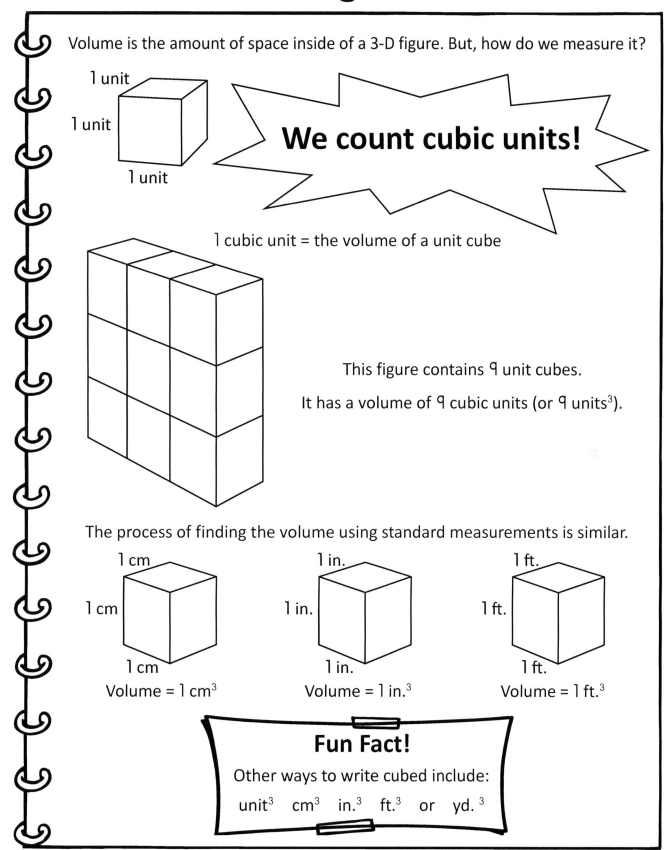

Volume is the amount of space inside of a 3-D figure. But, how do we measure it?

1 unit
1 unit
1 unit

We count cubic units!

1 cubic unit = the volume of a unit cube

This figure contains 9 unit cubes.

It has a volume of 9 cubic units (or 9 units^3).

The process of finding the volume using standard measurements is similar.

1 cm
1 cm
1 cm
Volume = 1 cm^3

1 in.
1 in.
1 in.
Volume = 1 in.^{3}

1 ft.
1 ft.
1 ft.
Volume = 1 ft.^{3}

Fun Fact!

Other ways to write cubed include:

unit^3 cm^3 in.^{3} ft.^{3} or   yd.^{3}

Name: _____

Measuring Volume

Work with your partner to solve these practice problems.

For questions 1–4, count the number of cubes to find the volume.

1.

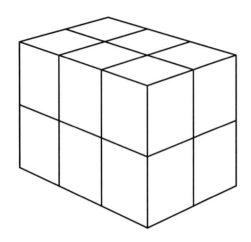

_____ cubic units

2.

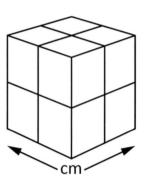

cm

_____ cubic cm

3.

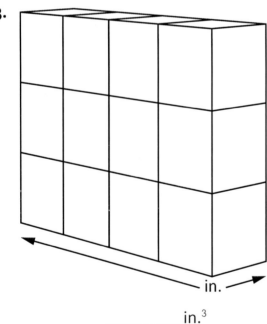

in.

_____ in.^{3}

4.

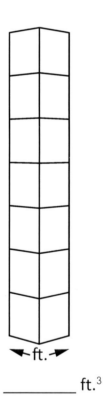

ft.

_____ ft.^{3}

5. How can the figures in problems 1 and 3 both have the same volume?

_____

_____

Name: _____

Measuring Volume

Focus on what you learned. Find the answers.

For questions 1–4, count the number of cubes to find the volume.

1.

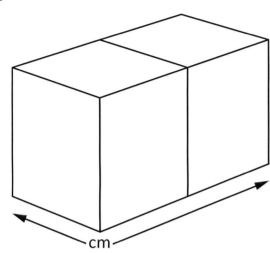

_____ cm³

2.

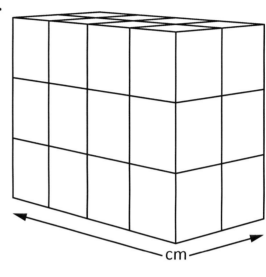

_____ cm³

3.

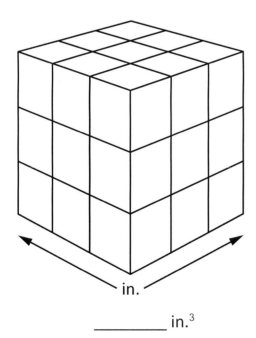

_____ in.³

4.

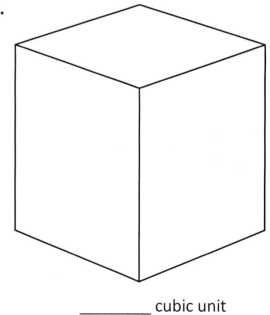

_____ cubic unit

5. A rectangular prism contains 50 unit cubes. What is its volume?

_____

Name: _____

Measuring Volume

Think about measuring volume. Write about what you learned.

1. Draw a rectangular prism that has a volume of 10 cubic units.

2. Philip counted the faces of cubes on three sides of the following prism. Then he multiplied the numbers to get a volume of 576 cubic units. What did he do wrong? What is the volume of this prism?

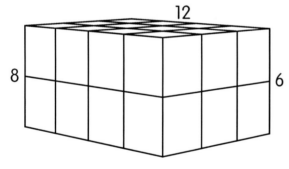

$$\begin{array}{r} 12 \\ \times\ \ 8 \\ \hline 96 \\ \times\ \ \ \ 6 \\ \hline 576 \end{array}$$

_____

_____

3. The important thing to remember about measuring volume is _____

_____

_____

_____

Name: _____

$$V = l \times w \times h$$

We know how to find the volume of a rectangular prism by counting cubes.

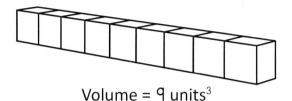

Volume = 9 units^3

But sometimes, it's hard to count the number of unit cubes in a figure.

That's when we can turn to a formula!

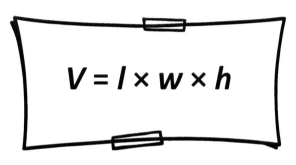

$$V = l \times w \times h$$

To find the volume of a rectangular prism, we multiply the length by the width by the height.

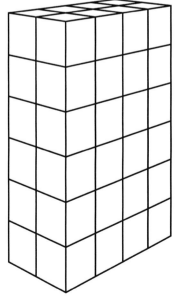

4 cm × 2 cm × 6 cm = 48 cm^3

The volume of the rectangular prism is 48 cm^3.

Name: _____

$$V = l \times w \times h$$

Work with your partner to solve these practice problems.

Find the volume of the following rectangular prisms.

1.

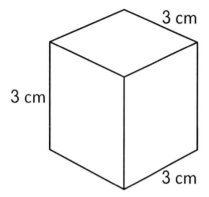

3 cm

3 cm

3 cm

_____

2.

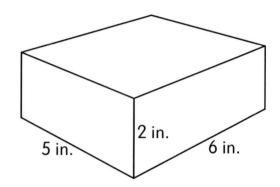

2 in.

5 in.

6 in.

_____

3.

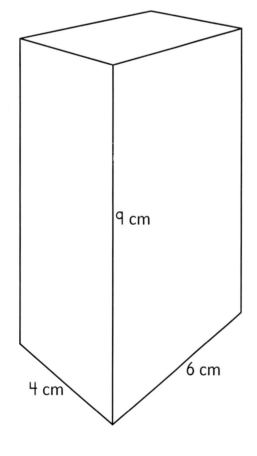

9 cm

6 cm

4 cm

_____

4.

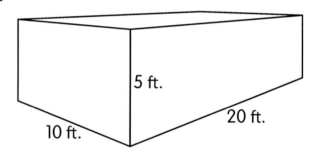

5 ft.

10 ft.

20 ft.

_____

5.

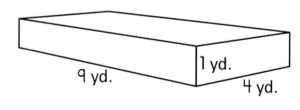

1 yd.

9 yd.

4 yd.

_____

Geometric Measurements

Name: _____

$$V = l \times w \times h$$

Focus on what you learned. Find the answers.

1. What is the volume of a rectangular prism whose length is 5 cm, width is 3 cm, and height is 4 cm?

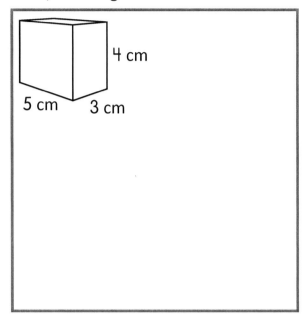

2. A swimming pool is 10 ft. long by 20 ft. wide and 6 ft. deep. What is its volume?

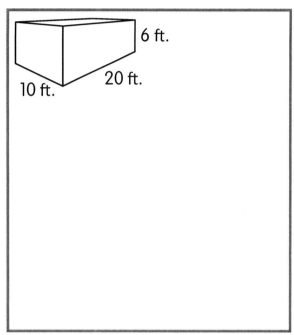

3. Fill in the blank number.

$$32 \text{ in.}^3 = 4 \text{ in.} \times 2 \text{ in.} \times \underline{\hspace{1.5cm}}$$

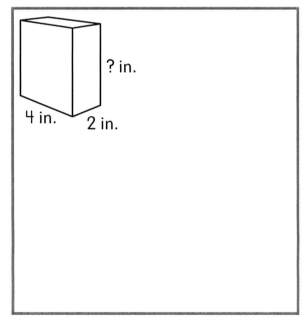

4. Draw a rectangular prism with the following dimensions. Length = 5 cm, Width = 3 cm, Height = 2 cm.

5. What is the volume for the figure you drew in question 4? _____

Name: _____

$V = l \times w \times h$

Think about the formula $V = l \times w \times h$. Write about what you learned.

1. The volume of a rectangular prism is 54 yd.^{3}. What is one possible set of dimensions for the prism? Write or draw and label your response below.

_____

_____

_____

2. Write a word problem in which you would use the volume formula to find the answer. Then solve the problem and show your work on the back of this sheet.

_____

_____

3. I feel (confident/confused) about using the formula for volume because _____

_____

_____

_____

Name: _____

$$V = b \times h$$

One formula for finding the volume of a rectangular prism is $V = l \times w \times h$.

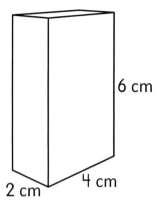

6 cm

2 cm   4 cm

2 cm × 4 cm × 6 cm = 48 cm^3

Another way to find the volume of a rectangular prism is to multiply the area of the base (*b*) times the height (*h*).

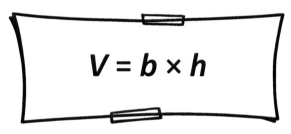

$$V = b \times h$$

First, find the base area.

Area = the amount of space *inside* a 2-D object.

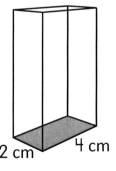

2 cm   4 cm

2 cm × 4 cm = 8 cm^2

The area of the base is 8 cm^2.

Then, multiply the base area times the height.

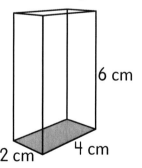

6 cm

2 cm   4 cm

8 cm × 6 cm = 48 cm^3

The volume of the rectangular prism is 48 cm^3.

Name: _____

$V = b \times h$

Work with your partner to solve these practice problems.

1. The base area of a rectangular prism is 33 cm². Its height is 2 cm. What is the prism's volume?

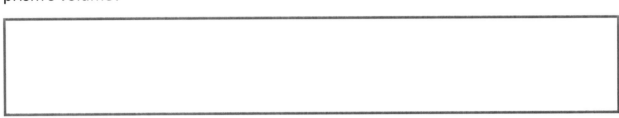

2. A rectangular prism has a base area of 40 in.². Its height is 4 in. What is its volume?

3. If the base area of a rectangular prism is 8 ft.² and the volume is 64 ft.³, what is its height?

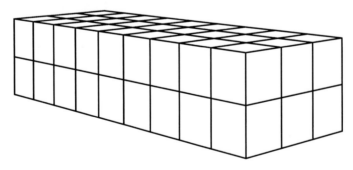

4. Find the base area for the figure above. _____

5. Using the formula $V = b \times h$, what is the volume of the figure above? _____

Name: _____

$$V = b \times h$$

Focus on what you learned. Find the answers. Complete the chart.

	Length (*l*)	Width (*w*)	Height (*h*)	Area of Base (*b = l × w*)	Volume (*V = b × h*)
1.	2 cm	2 cm	2 cm		
2.	3 in.	1 in.	4 in.		
3.	5 ft.	2 ft.	3 ft.		
4.	8 cm			16 cm^2	16 cm^3
5.	3 in.		2 in.	9 in.^{2}	

Name: _____

$$V = b \times h$$

Think about the formula $V = b \times h$. Write about what you learned.

1. How is $V = l \times w \times h$ similar to $V = b \times h$?

_____

_____

_____

2. How does having a formula help to find the volume of a rectangular prism?

_____

_____

_____

3. One question I still have about finding volume is _____

_____

_____

Name: _____

Decimal Word Problems

When solving word problems, follow the five steps below.

Let's try solving a problem!

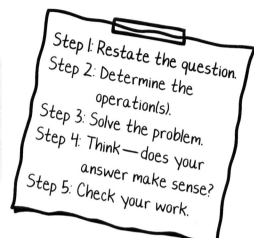

Step 1: Restate the question.
Step 2: Determine the operation(s).
Step 3: Solve the problem.
Step 4: Think—does your answer make sense?
Step 5: Check your work.

Elena bought $3.48 worth of grapes. Nima bought $2.25 worth of energy bars. Wendy bought 2 bags of apples at $6.99 each. How much did the girls spend in all?

Step 1: Restate the question.

How much did the girls spend?

Step 2: Determine the operation(s).

The question asks to find the total amount, so I will need to add.

Step 3: Solve the problem.

$3.48 + $2.25 + $6.99 + $6.99 = $19.71

Step 4: Think—does your answer make sense?

If I estimate $3.50 + $2.25 + $14 = $19.75, then $19.71 makes sense.

Step 5: Check your work.

$19.71 − $13.98 − $2.25 = $3.48

Name: _____

Decimal Word Problems

Work with your partner to solve these practice problems.

1. Shen is building a storage shelf to hold supply boxes. Each box is 12.55 inches wide. He has 7 boxes. How long does his shelf need to be?

Step 1: Restate the question.

_____

_____

Step 2: Determine the operation(s).

_____

Step 3: Solve the problem.

Step 4: Think—does your answer make sense?

_____

Step 5: Check your work.

2. Mr. Solazzo's class took a field trip to the art museum. Each ticket cost $6.65. The total bill was $139.65. How many students went on the field trip?

Step 1: Restate the question.

_____

_____

Step 2: Determine the operation(s).

_____

Step 3: Solve the problem.

Step 4: Think—does your answer make sense?

_____

Step 5: Check your work.

Name: _____

Decimal Word Problems

Focus on what you learned. Find the answers.

1. Umi brought a new puppy to the vet's office. The puppy weighed 5.26 pounds. At a checkup three months later, it weighed 11.65 pounds. How much weight did the puppy gain?

   Step 1: Restate the question.

   _____

   _____

   Step 2: Determine the operation(s).

   _____

   Step 3: Solve the problem.

   Step 4: Think—does your answer make sense?

   _____

   Step 5: Check your work.

2. Tovah got a job earning $10.25/hour. She worked 8 hours on Monday. How much did she earn for the day?

   Step 1: Restate the question.

   _____

   _____

   Step 2: Determine the operation(s).

   _____

   Step 3: Solve the problem.

   Step 4: Think—does your answer make sense?

   _____

   Step 5: Check your work.

THINK & WRITE

Name: _____

Decimal Word Problems

Think about solving decimal word problems. Write about what you learned.

1. Saul's drone is 10.02 cm tall. His sister's drone is 5.68 cm tall. He wants to know how much taller his drone is. What should he do to find out? Why?

_____

_____

_____

_____

2. Write a decimal word problem that requires subtraction. Solve it.

_____

_____

_____

**READ &
LEARN**

Name: _____

Fraction Word Problems

When solving word problems with fractions, follow the five steps below to find the answer.

> After Thanksgiving, Grandpa had $\frac{1}{2}$ of an apple pie left over. The next day, Gabby ate $\frac{1}{5}$ of it. How much of the whole pie did Gabby eat?

Step 1: Restate the question.
Step 2: Determine the operation(s).
Step 3: Solve the problem.
Step 4: Think—does your answer make sense?
Step 5: Check your work.

Step 1: Restate the question.

How much of the whole pie did Gabby eat?

Step 2: Determine the operation(s).

The question asks to find a part of a whole, so I will need to multiply.

Step 3: Solve the problem.

$\frac{1}{5} \times \frac{1}{2} = \frac{1}{10}$. Gabby ate $\frac{1}{10}$ of the pie.

Step 4: Think—does your answer make sense?

Gabby would have eaten less than $\frac{1}{2}$ because that's all that was left. And, the answer should be less than $\frac{1}{5}$ because it was less than a full pie. Therefore, $\frac{1}{10}$ makes sense.

Step 5: Check your work.

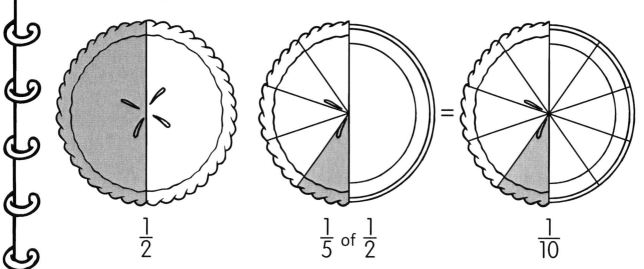

$$\frac{1}{2} \qquad \frac{1}{5} \text{ of } \frac{1}{2} \qquad \frac{1}{10}$$

Name: _____

Fraction Word Problems

Work with your partner to solve these practice problems.

1. Archie and Carter are comparing their bug collections. Archie's biggest bug is $\frac{5}{7}$ of an inch. Carter's biggest bug is $\frac{3}{4}$ of an inch. How much bigger is Carter's bug than Archie's?

2. The grocery store has 52 pies, and $\frac{1}{4}$ of them are blueberry. The bakery has 20 pies and $\frac{1}{2}$ of them are blueberry. Does the grocery store or the bakery have more blueberry pies?

Name: _____

Fraction Word Problems

Focus on what you learned. Find the answers.

1. Carlo and Jamal are hiking with their families. The trail is 2 miles long. They hiked $\frac{3}{4}$ of a mile before they took their first break. They hiked $\frac{2}{3}$ of a mile more before taking another break. How much farther do they have to hike before they complete the trail?

2. Maria and Virginia have 3 bags of granola. They want to serve their friends $\frac{1}{6}$ bag of granola each. How many friends can they serve?

Fraction Word Problems

Think about fraction word problems. Write about what you learned.

1. Adam ate $\frac{2}{3}$ of the pizza his father ordered for him. His father ate $\frac{5}{7}$ of what was left. How would you figure out what fraction of the original pizza Adam's father ate?

2. How do you know when to use multiplication when solving a fraction word problem?

_____

_____

_____

Name: _____

Conversion Word Problems

When completing word problems that require us to convert standard measurements, we need to remember basic conversions.

> 1 foot = 12 inches
> 1 yard = 3 feet
> 1 mile = 1,760 yards

> 8 ounces = 1 cup
> 2 cups = 1 pint
> 2 pints = 1 quart

Let's solve a problem!

> When Charlie was born, she was 20 inches long. When she entered fifth grade, she was 4 ft., 6 in. long. How many inches has she grown?

We need to convert feet to inches.

$$4 \times 12 = 48$$

Then, we need to add the extra 6 inches.

$$48 + 6 = 54$$

Charlie was 54 inches when she started fifth grade.

Now, we need to subtract the 20 inches from when she was born.

$$54 - 20 = 34$$

Charlie has grown 34 inches.

Don't forget...
- *When converting larger units to smaller units, multiply.*
- *When converting smaller units to larger units, divide.*

Step 1: Restate the question.
Step 2: Determine the operation(s).
Step 3: Solve the problem.
Step 4: Think—does your answer make sense?
Step 5: Check your work.

Name: _____

Conversion Word Problems

Work with your partner to solve these practice problems.

1. Luez ate 3 pints of strawberries. How many cups did he eat?

2. Sienna needs $\frac{3}{4}$ yard of fabric to make a blanket for her stuffed animal. She finds 2 feet of fabric. Does she have enough? Explain your reasoning.

Conversion Word Problems

Focus on what you learned. Find the answers.

1. Cooper bought 5 quarts of ice cream for his party. Twenty of his friends are coming. He wants to serve each friend 1 cup of ice cream. Can he do this? Why, or why not?

2. Shalini and her sister Priyanka ran 5,984 yards. How many miles did they run?

Name: _____

Conversion Word Problems

Think about conversion word problems. Write about what you learned.

1. How do you know whether you need to multiply or divide when converting standard measurements in word problems?

_____

_____

_____

_____

2. Mr. Jones asked his fifth-graders how many inches are in 5 pints. His students could not answer him. Why not?

_____

_____

_____

_____

Answer Key

Page 6
1. 52   2. 21   3. 12

Page 7
1. 36   2. 48
3. Answers will vary. One solution is $4 + \{12 - [1 + (3 + 2)]\}$.
4. Answers will vary. One solution is $4 + \{8 + 2[(3 + 2) + 1]\}$.

Challenge: Answers will vary. Accept all accurately solved problems that have two sets of parentheses, one set of brackets, and one set of braces.

Page 8
1. Answers will vary but may include: I need to solve the problem in the parentheses first, then the brackets, and then the braces.
2. Torriana started off correctly with the parentheses (4−1), but then she subtracted 1 instead of multiplying by 4. She made the mistake with the basic order of operations (PEMDAS). The correct answer should be 0.
3. Answers will vary.

Page 10
1. $20(5 - 2)$
2. $(50 \div 10) + 20(5 - 2)$
3. $(20 + 10) \div 5$
4. 4
5. three times the difference of sixty and four

Page 11
1. $23(3 + 16 + 50)$
2. $3(6 \div 2)$
3. Fifty-two times the difference of five-hundred fifteen and twenty-four
4. Answers will vary but may include: $(515 - 24) \div 4$ is one-fourth of $515 - 24$
5. $(20 + 6 + 6) \div 3$

Page 12
1. $50(2 + 7 + 5)$. Answers for explanation will vary but should include references to the order of operations.
2. Answers will vary. Accept all that accurately represent $12 - (2 \times 3 - 4)$.
3. Answers will vary.

Page 14
1. 5,352,107
2. 3 hundreds
3. 5,555,555
4. The ten thousands place will decrease by 7, making the whole number less by 70,000.
5. 3,000,000

Page 15
1.

millions	hundred thousands	ten thousands	thousands	hundreds	tens	ones

2. the millions place
3. 5 hundred thousands
4. The thousands place will decrease by 1, making the whole number less by 1,000.
5. 600,095

Page 16
1. Answers will vary but should support the concept of the base-ten number system.
2. 225,890   3,256,421
I know because if you put the digits in a place value chart, these two numbers have a 2 in the hundred thousands place.
3. Answers will vary.

Page 18
1. $4 \times 1 + 2(\frac{1}{10}) + 5(\frac{1}{100}) + 4(\frac{1}{1000})$
2. 3.701
3. ten and two hundred sixty-eight thousandths
4.

0	.	4	0	3

5. thirty-two hundredths or $3(\frac{1}{10}) + 2(\frac{1}{100})$

Page 19
1. 5.16
2. 9.300
3. $4 \times 1 + 1(\frac{1}{10}) + 6(\frac{1}{100})$
4. $5(\frac{1}{10}) + 1(\frac{1}{100}) + 5(\frac{1}{1000})$
5. 9.235

Page 20
1. There are 1,000 thousandths in 1. Answers will vary but should reference the base-ten number system. Since 10 tenths equals 1, then 100 hundredths would equal 1, and 1,000 thousandths would equal 1.
2. *And* stands for the decimal point. It helps identify where whole-number values end and decimal values begin.
3. Answers will vary.

Page 22
1. 5   3. 4.6   5. 4.67
2. 5   4. 4.0   6. 6.00

Page 23
1. 6.1   3. 7.22   5. 8.2
2. 7.1   4. 6.07   inches

Page 24
1. Answers will vary but may include: Number lines allow me to put numbers in organized spots to show me which way I should round.
2. 15.7. Answers will vary—accept all reasonable responses.
3. Answers will vary.

Page 26
1. >   2. >   3. =
4. 4.540, 4.570, 4.892

Page 27
1. >   2. >   3. <
4. Ariel did not organize her shell collection correctly. Explanations will vary but should recognize that 0.225 cm is bigger than 0.22 cm. Students might point out that Ariel could have added a 0 in the thousandths column to help her identify this.

Page 28
1.

Sunday	0.00 in.
Tuesday	0.5 in.
Friday	1.0 in.
Monday	1.21 in.
Saturday	1.25 in.
Thursday	2.25 in.
Wednesday	4.2 in.

2. Buffalo had the least amount of snow on Sunday. It had the greatest amount of snow on Wednesday. I know this because I ordered the digits according to place value and lined up the numbers, comparing digits of the same place value from left to right. 0.00 in. < 4.20 in.
3. Answers will vary.

Page 30
1. 6.44   3. 16.98   5. 19.34
2. 9.79   4. 5.79

Page 31
1. 1.89   3. 7.77   5. $28.24
2. 4.87   4. 5.87

Answer Key *(cont.)*

Page 32
1. Answers will vary but one important suggestion would be to make sure he lines up the decimal point. The correct answer should be 12.35.
2. Yes, the girls have enough sugar for the recipe. 1.6 + 0.6 = 2.2, so they have more than the necessary 2 cups of sugar to bake cupcakes.
3. Answers will vary.

Page 34
1. 3.5
2. 12.4
3. 2.95
4. 3.77
5. $11.25

Page 35
1. 1.75
2. 0.08
3. 3.24
4. 3.25
5. $0.40 or 40¢

Page 36
1. Student answers will vary. They may write about place value, dropping the decimal point, or adding 0s in empty place holders.
2. Student answers will vary but may include: 14.59 − 12.01 is 2.58 while 3.01 − 0.06 = 2.95, so 2.58 is less than 2.95.
3. Answers will vary.

Page 38
1. 16.1538
2. 0.1125
3. 16.3212
4. 6 × 13.2 = 79.2 oz.

Page 39
1. 0.21
2. 6.4
3. 56
4. 231.684
5. Answers will vary.

Page 40
1. Answers will vary. One possibility includes: You multiply whole numbers and decimals the same way by lining up numbers in their place value spots. Multiplying decimals is different because you have to count over the number of decimal places.
2. 2.52. You could find the answer counting the decimals and "hopping" over the same number of places.
3. Answers will vary.

Page 42
1. 10
2. 280
3. 52
4. 1.5
5. 26.75
6. 25.6

Page 43
1. 2
2. 4.8
3. 5
4. 99
5. 2.5
6. 6.2

Page 44
1. Answers will vary but will likely include the explanation that it is easier to divide whole numbers than decimals.
2. Both problems would give you the same answer because if you convert the divisors to whole numbers by using a multiple of ten, you end up with the same problem.
3. Answers will vary.

Page 46
1. $^{29}/_{35}$
2. $^{15}/_{30}$ or $^{1}/_{2}$
3. $^{11}/_{24}$
4. $^{11}/_{15}$
5. Drawings will vary. The answer should be $^{5}/_{8}$.

Page 47
1. $^{11}/_{12}$
2. $^{5}/_{6}$
3. $^{66}/_{90}$ or $^{11}/_{15}$
4. $^{7}/_{8}$
5. $^{13}/_{15}$

Page 48
1. $^{1}/_{5}$. Answers will vary but should include changing to equivalent fractions so the denominator is 15. Thus, $^{3}/_{15} + ^{3}/_{15} = ^{6}/_{15}$.
2. Answers will vary but should explain how to use equivalent fractions to form a common denominator and then add.
3. Answers will vary.

Page 50
1. $^{7}/_{12}$
2. $^{11}/_{42}$
3. $^{14}/_{40}$ or $^{7}/_{20}$
4. $^{4}/_{12}$ or $^{1}/_{3}$
5. $^{13}/_{24}$
6. $^{4}/_{35}$

Page 51
1. $^{1}/_{8}$
2. $^{5}/_{36}$
3. $^{11}/_{18}$
4. $^{9}/_{16}$
5. $^{8}/_{21}$
6. $^{1}/_{10}$

Page 52
1. Timothy is right. $^{1}/_{3} - ^{2}/_{5}$ converts to $^{5}/_{15} - ^{6}/_{15}$. So, Jeff did not have enough string to use $^{2}/_{5}$ of a yard.
2. Joanna is not correct. 39 is not a common denominator of both 13 and 26. The correct answer is $^{5}/_{26}$.
3. Answers will vary.

Page 54
1. $^{15}/_{24}$ or $^{5}/_{8}$
2. $^{7}/_{30}$
3. $^{8}/_{72}$ or $^{1}/_{9}$
4. $^{1}/_{40}$
5. $^{20}/_{77}$

Page 55
1. e
2. a
3. c
4. d
5. b

Page 56
1. Answers will vary, but may include: When multiplying fractions, the numbers get smaller. You need to multiply the numerators and denominators and then simplify if necessary.
2. Answers will vary. Make sure the product has been reduced.
3. Answers will vary.

Page 58
1. 7 × $^{3}/_{4}$
2. $^{3}/_{4} + ^{3}/_{4} + ^{3}/_{4} + ^{3}/_{4} + ^{3}/_{4} + ^{3}/_{4} + ^{3}/_{4} = ^{21}/_{4}$ or $5^{1}/_{4}$
3. $^{7}/_{1} × ^{3}/_{4} = ^{21}/_{4}$ or $5^{1}/_{4}$
4. $^{24}/_{7}$ or $3^{3}/_{7}$
5. $^{18}/_{3}$ or 6

Page 59
1. $^{25}/_{6}$ or $4^{1}/_{6}$
2. $^{33}/_{5}$ or $6^{3}/_{5}$
3. $^{14}/_{8} = ^{7}/_{4}$ or $1^{3}/_{4}$
4. $^{77}/_{14} = ^{11}/_{2}$ or $5^{1}/_{2}$
5. Answers will vary. Accept all answers that show 3 groups with 1 of 4 items shaded.

Page 60
1. The figure shows 6 groups, with $^{1}/_{5}$ of the groups shaded. So, it represents 6 × $^{1}/_{5}$.
2. Jamie is correct because if you multiply a number by a fraction, you are taking a part of it. By multiplying by 1, you always get the same amount. When multiplying by more than 1, you get a multiple of that amount. When multiplying by a fraction, you get a portion of the original amount.
3. Answers will vary.

Page 62
1. 8
2. 10
3. $^{12}/_{5}$ or $2^{2}/_{5}$
4. $^{40}/_{9}$ or $4^{4}/_{9}$
5. 18
6. 56

Page 63
1. $^{24}/_{5}$ or $4^{4}/_{5}$
2. 10
3. 18
4. $^{3}/_{2}$ or $1^{1}/_{2}$
5. $^{1}/_{2}$

Riddle: Gymnasts would like #2 best because it's a perfect score!

Page 64
1. The answer is always more than the original when you divide a whole number by a fraction because we're trying to figure out how many parts of something can fit into the whole—that's always going to be more than the original whole number.
2. Answers will vary. Accept all reasonable responses.
3. Answers will vary.

Answer Key *(cont.)*

Page 66
1. 1.5 feet
2. 12 yards
3. 5,280 feet
4. 1,164 inches
5. 8 cups
6. 3 quarts
7. 64 ounces
8. 328 ounces

Page 67
1. 36 inches
2. 3 miles
3. 10,560 feet
4. 2 yards
5. 3 cups
6. ½ cup
7. 4 cups
8. 656 cups

Page 68
1. When converting inches to yards, you need to divide because inches are smaller units than yards. When converting larger units to smaller units, multiply, and when converting smaller units to larger units, divide.
2. The playground that is 0.5 miles long is longer because 1 mile = 1,760 yards. 0.5 miles = 880 yards. Therefore, 0.5 miles (880 yards) is larger than 100 yards.
3. Answers will vary.

Page 70
1. ½, 1¾, 2, 2½, 2½, 2¾, 3
2.

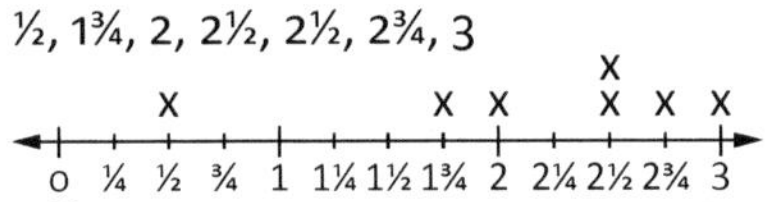

```
                      x
    x         x x   x x x
o   ¼  ½  ¾  1  1¼ 1½ 1¾  2  2¼ 2½ 2¾  3
```
3. 2 ½
4. 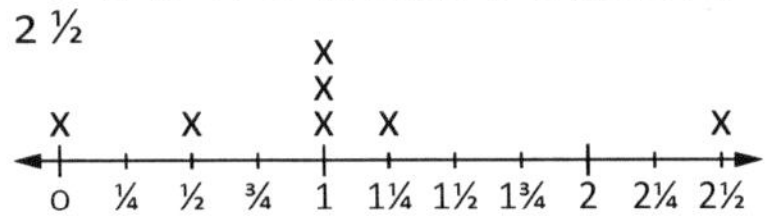
```
        x
        x
    x   x  x
x   x   x  x           x
o   ¼  ½  ¾  1  1¼ 1½ 1¾  2  2¼ 2½
```
5. Answers will vary. One possibility is "Rainfall for Jupiter, FL for One Week"

Page 71
1. 3, 3¼, 3¾, 4, 4, 4½, 4¾, 5, 5
2. 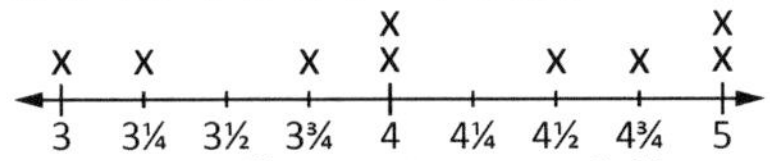
```
                x              x
                x              x
    x   x       x   x    x  x  x
3   3¼  3½  3¾  4  4¼  4½  4¾   5
```
3. Answers will vary. One possibility is: Distance (in feet) Mrs. Hader's Students Jumped.
4. 1 more student jumped 5 feet than 3 feet.

Page 72
1. Organizing data before plotting it makes it easier to see how many dots or Xs you need to put on the line. It also makes it less likely to make a mistake.
2. Line plots with whole numbers don't need additional measures on the ruler or horizontal scale to identify the appropriate unit (such as halves or quarters).
3. Answers will vary.

Page 74
1. square
2. rhombus
3. acute triangle
4. parallelogram
5. right triangle
6. rectangle

Page 75
1. Figure should have 3 sides + 3 acute angles.
2. Figure should have 4 equal sides + 4 right angles.
3. Figure should have 2 parallel sides and 2 opposite equal angles.
4. Figure should have 3 sides + 1 right angle.
5. Figure should have 4 sides + 4 right angles.
6. Figure should have 3 sides + 1 obtuse angle.

Page 76
1. Answers will vary but should refer to counting the number of sides and identifying the angles to match the description of the various 2-D figures.
2. An acute triangle is one in which all angles are less than 90 degrees, whereas an obtuse triangle has one angle that is greater than 90 degrees.
3. Answers will vary.

Page 78
1. rhombus
2. oval
3. trapezoid
4. square
5. triangle

Defy Gravity: a star should be at (9, 9)

Page 79
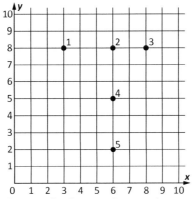

Flying High: The coordinate pairs connect to create the letter *T*.

Page 80
1. Answers will vary but can include plotting the first number on the *x*-axis and the second number on the *y*-axis.
2. Lisa is confused about which number in a coordinate pair belongs to which axis. The first number shows how far to travel along the *x*-axis, while the second shows how far to travel on the *y*-axis.
3. Answers will vary.

Page 82
1.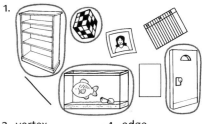
2. vertex
3. face
4. edge
5. 6

Page 83
1.
2. Cube: 6 faces, 12 edges, and 8 vertices.
3. Rectangular Prism: 6 faces, 12 edges, and 8 vertices.
4. Triangular Prism: 5 faces, 9 edges, and 6 vertices.

Page 84
1. Cup B has the greater volume because it has more space to hold liquid.
2. Rectangular prisms and cubes always have the same number of faces, edges, and vertices because a cube is a kind of rectangular prism. Both cubes and rectangular prisms have 6 faces, 12 edges, and 8 vertices. The faces on cubes are all the same size.
3. Answers will vary.

Page 86
1. 12
2. 8
3. 12
4. 7
5. They both have the same number of unit cubes.

Page 87
1. 2
2. 24
3. 27
4. 1
5. 50 cubic units

Answer Key *(cont.)*

Page 88
1. Answers will vary. Accept all answers that contain 10 unit cubes. One possibility is:

2. Philip should have counted the unit cubes. The volume for this prism is 24 cubic units.
3. Answers will vary.

Page 90
1. 27 cm^3
2. 60 in.^{3}
3. 216 cm^3
4. 1,000 ft.^{3}
5. 36 yd.^{3}

Page 91
1. 60 cm^3
2. 1,200 ft.^{3}
3. 4 in.
4.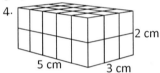
5. 30 cm^3

Page 92
1. Answers will vary. Some possible solutions include 27 yd. × 2 yd. × 1 yd., 9 yd. × 3 yd. × 2 yd.
2. Answers will vary.
3. Answers will vary.

Page 94
1. 66 cm^3
2. 160 in.^{3}
3. 8 ft.
4. 27 units^2
5. 54 units^3

Page 95

	Length	Width	Height	Area of Base	Volume
1.	2 cm	2 cm	2 cm	4 cm^2	8 cm^3
2.	3 in.	1 in.	4 in.	3 in.^{2}	12 in.^{3}
3.	5 ft.	2 ft.	3 ft.	10 ft.^{2}	30 ft.^{3}
4.	8 cm	2 cm	1 cm	16 cm^2	16 cm^3
5.	3 in.	3 in.	2 in.	9 in.^{2}	18 in.^{3}

Page 96
1. $V = l \times w \times h$ is similar to $V = b \times h$ because base area = $l \times w$, and when we multiply that by height, we're finding the same measurement.
2. Answers will vary. One option could be that a formula saves time. Counting cubes can be tricky, especially when you can't see all of them.
3. Answers will vary.

Page 98
1. How long does the shelf need to be to hold 7 boxes? I will need to use multiplication; 12.55 × 7 = 87.85. The shelf needs to be at least 87.85 inches long. 7 × 13 = 91, so that answer makes sense. 87.85 ÷ 7 = 12.55. The answer checks out.
2. How many students went on the field trip? I need to use division; 139.65 ÷ 6.65 = 21. Twenty-one students went on the field trip.; This answer makes sense—it's about the size of a typical class. Plus, 21 × 7 = 147, so that's close. To check, 21 × 6.65 = 139.65.

Page 99
1. How much weight did the puppy gain? I need to use subtraction; 11.65 − 5.26 = 6.39. The puppy gained 6.39 pounds. This makes sense because 12 − 5 = 7, so the answer should be around 7. 6.39 + 5.26 = 11.65. The answer checks out.
2. How much will Tovah earn? I will need to use multiplication; 10.25 × 8 = 82. She will earn $82 for the day. 10 × 8 = 80, so the answer makes sense. 82 ÷ 8 = 10.25. The answer checks out.

Page 100
1. Answers will vary. Students can write about the 5 steps: Restate the question, Determine what operation you will use to solve the problem, Solve the problem, Think—does your answer make sense?; and Check your work. They can also draw pictures to explain what they would do and/or describe how to solve the problem.
2. Answers will vary.

Page 102
1. Carter's bug is ¹⁄₂₈ of an inch bigger than Archie's.
2. The grocery store has more blueberry pies. (The grocery store has 13, and the bakery has 10.)

Page 103
1. The boys need to hike ⁷⁄₁₂ more miles.
2. Maria and Virginia can serve 18 friends.

Page 104
1. Answers will vary. They can write about the 5 steps: Restate the question, Determine what operation you will use to solve the problem, Solve the problem, Think—does your answer make sense?; and Check your work. They can also draw pictures to explain what they would do and/or describe how to solve the problem. They can also plug in numbers. For example, if tvhere were 21 pizza slices to begin with, then Adam ate 14, and his father ate 5 of the remaining 7. So, Adam's father ate ¹⁰⁄₂₁ of the original pizza.
2. Answers will vary but should address the word choice in the problem. For example, if determining a repeated distance of time (3 hours of 0.5 miles), combining equal-numbered groups (6 groups of ⅔ bowl), or finding a part of a part (¼ of ⅔), they should multiply the fractions.

Page 106
1. Luez ate 6 cups of strawberries.
2. Sienna does not have enough fabric. 2 ft. = ⅔ yd. ⅔ yd. is less than ¾ yd. (⅔ = ⁸⁄₁₂ and ¾ = ⁹⁄₁₂).

Page 107
1. Cooper will have exactly 20 cups of ice cream. He can serve each of his friends 1 cup.
2. The girls ran 3.4 miles (5,984 ÷ 1,760 = 3.4)

Page 108
1. When solving word problems that involve converting standard measurements, you need to determine what you're converting. If the question asks you to convert larger units to smaller units, multiply. If the question asks you to convert smaller units to larger units, divide.
2. Mr. Jones's students could not answer him because inches measure length and pints measure volume. You cannot convert between these two types of measurement because they're different types of measurement—length is one-dimensional and volume is three-dimensional.